CAT

meow meow

LIFE CYCLES

Words that look like **this** can be found in the glossary on page 24.

©2018
Book Life
King's Lynn
Norfolk PE30 4LS

ISBN: 978-1-78637-235-2

Written by:
Holly Duhig
Edited by:
Kirsty Holmes
Designed by:
Danielle Jones

A catalogue record for this book is available from the British Library.

CAT

WHAT IS A LIFE CYCLE?

All animals, plants and humans go through different stages of their life as they grow and change. This is called a life cycle.

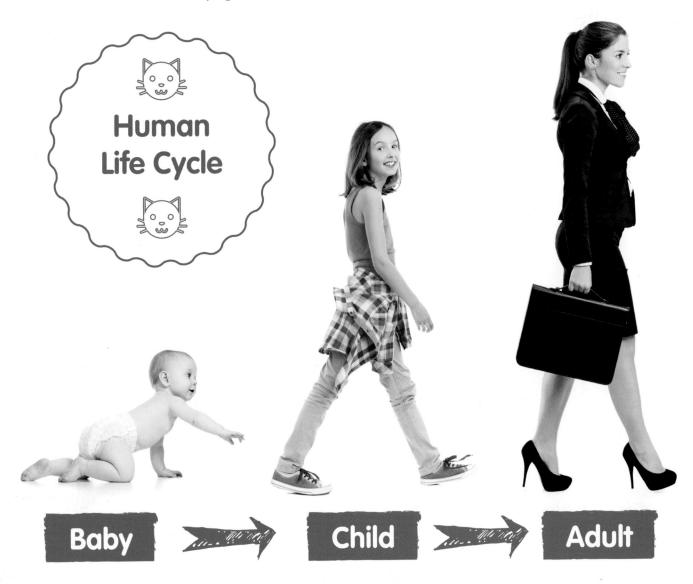

Human Life Cycle

Baby → **Child** → **Adult**

WHAT IS A CAT?

A cat is a **species** of **mammal**. They have lots of fur and **flexible** bodies. People often keep cats as pets because they are cute and friendly.

Pet Cat

KITTENS

A female cat will be **pregnant** for around 64 days before giving birth to kittens. She will normally find somewhere warm and dark to give birth.

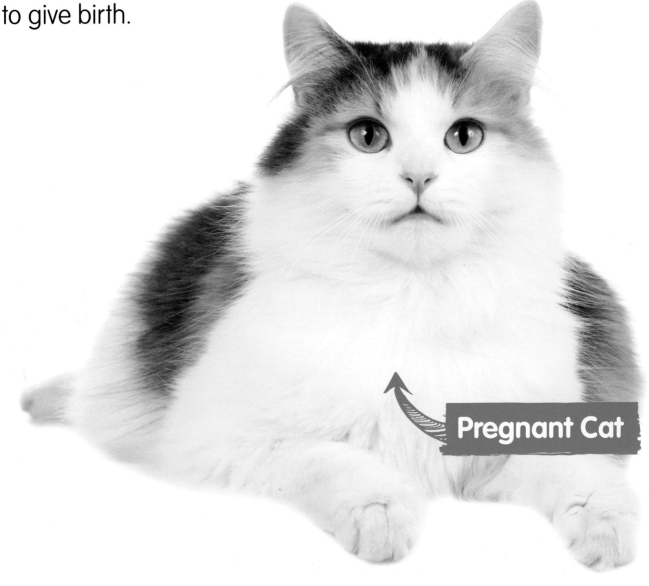

Pregnant Cat

Kittens are born blind and deaf.

A kitten is a young cat. An adult cat will usually give birth to about two to five kittens. This is called a litter.

GROWING KITTENS

They also have to stay very close to their mother after they are born as they can't yet keep themselves warm.

Newborn kittens sleep for around 22 hours every day!

When kittens are born, they don't open their eyes straight away. They keep them closed for around seven days.

CHANGING KITTENS

All kittens are born with blue eyes. Their eyes only start to change colour when they are between three to six months of age.

Adult cats can have blue, brown, green or even amber eyes.

Two Kittens Hunting

Once kittens are a bit older they begin to leave their mother's side to explore the world. They often play **hunting** games with other kittens.

CATS

An adult kitten is called a cat. Cats often spend their time hunting, sleeping and **grooming** themselves. Cats hunt small birds and mice.

A male cat is called a tom. A female cat is called a queen. Their kittens will usually look like a mix of both of their parents.

Tom

Queen

DIFFERENT BREEDS

Siamese Cat

There are many different **breeds** of cat. Siamese cats are a breed of cat from Asia. They are cream-coloured with brown faces and feet.

The Manx cat is a breed of cat that has no tail. Most cats use their tails for balance. However, the Manx cat is able to live without one.

Manx Cat

CATS IN THE WILD

A group of lions is called a pride.

Lions, tigers and other similar animals also belong to the cat family. This is why lions and tigers are often called big cats.

Bobcats are a type of wildcat from North America. They are about twice the size of a **domestic** cat and they hunt much bigger animals, such as rabbits and chickens.

Bobcat

CAT FACTS

Egyptian Cat Statue

The ancient Egyptians believed cats were **sacred**.

Siberian Tiger

The largest member of the cat family is the Siberian tiger.
They can grow to around 3.5 metres long from nose to tail.

WORLD RECORD BREAKERS

Longest Whiskers in the World

The world record for the longest whiskers on a cat is held by Missi, whose whiskers measure 19 centimetres.

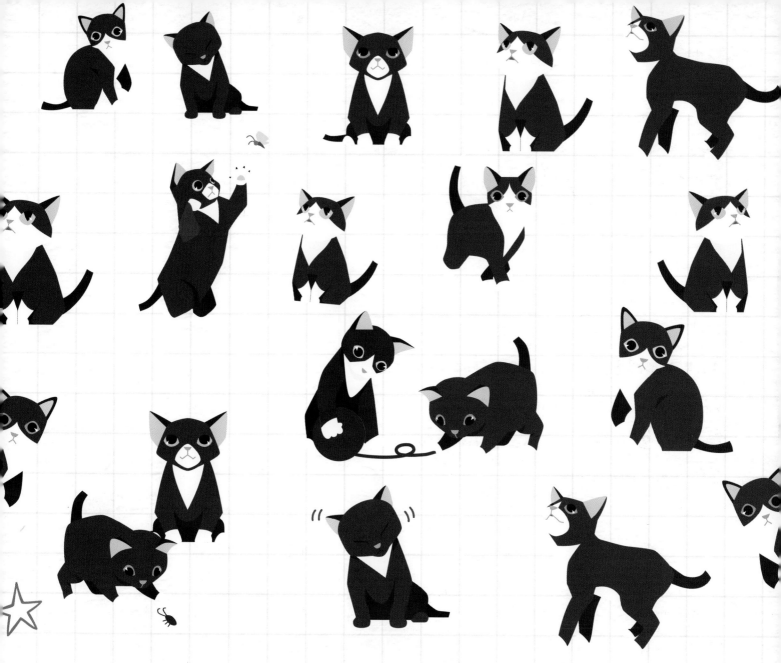

Largest Litter of Kittens

The record for the largest litter of kittens ever born was 19!
These kittens were born in Oxfordshire, UK, in 1970.

LIFE CYCLE OF A CAT

1 A female cat gives birth to a litter of kittens who are blind and deaf.

2 The kittens feed on their mother's milk until they are ready to hunt.

LIFE CYCLES

4 The kittens grow into adult cats.

3 The kittens' hearing and eyesight improves.

22

GET EXPLORING!

Do you, or any of your friends, own a cat? What colour is its fur?
Can you tell what breed it is?

GLOSSARY

breeds groups of animals in the same species that have similar characteristics

domestic tame and kept by humans

flexible easy to bend

grooming to brush and clean an animal's coat or fur

hunting to chase and kill wild animals for food or sport

mammal an animal that has warm blood, a backbone and produces milk

pregnant when a female develops a baby inside her

sacred connected to a god or gods

species a group of very similar animals or plants that are capable of producing young together

INDEX